THE SIZE OF A BIRD

The publisher gratefully acknowledges the support of the Canada Council for the Arts and the Ontario Arts Council for its publishing program. The publisher is also grateful for the financial assistance received from the Government of Canada.

Cover design: Cee Lavery

Library and Archives Canada Cataloguing in Publication

Morrigan, Clementine, 1986-, author
        The size of a bird / poems by Clementine Morrigan.

(Inanna poetry & fiction series)
Issued in print and electronic formats.
ISBN 978-1-77133-457-0 (softcover). -- ISBN 978-1-77133-458-7 (EPUB). --
ISBN 978-1-77133-459-4 (Kindle). -- ISBN 978-1-77133-460-0 (PDF)

        I. Title. II. Series: Inanna poetry and fiction series

PS8626.O7554S59 2017   C811'.6   C2017-905457-0
                                                C2017-905458-9

Printed and bound in Canada

Inanna Publications and Education Inc.
210 Founders College, York University
4700 Keele Street, Toronto, Ontario M3J 1P3 Canada
Telephone: (416) 736-5356   Fax (416) 736-5765
Email: inanna.publications@inanna.ca Website: www.inanna.ca

THE SIZE OF A BIRD

POETRY BY

CLEMENTINE MORRIGAN

inanna poetry & fiction series

INANNA Publications and Education Inc.
Toronto, Canada

ALSO BY CLEMENTINE MORRIGAN

Rupture

For Sam and for Angel

Contents

VIII: THE WORST THING

IX: UNBROKEN

1. WRITE A PLACE FOR THE PAIN

Write a Place for the Pain

Write. Find the words in your spine. Find the words in your fingers. Find the words which are not words which are sounds. Find the bathtub words, the swing set words, the words for grassy lawn laying. Find the words for break ups, broken hearts, getting on your knees and praying. Find the words for hope, laughter, running down sidewalks. Find the words that are choked up in the back of your throat, breathless. Find the words that ache in your gut. Find the words scrawled on the back of your hand so you won't forget.

Write. Find the words you wrote in a letter to your first girlfriend after she broke your heart, the words for the way you went back to your math class and lay your head flat on the desk, crying. Find the words for no, for not now, for not ever. Find the words for get off me, for I'll fucking kill you, find the words for never fucking touch me like that again. Find the words for I'm sorry, I miss you so much, I did the best I could. Find the words for long lost fantasies, what you thought would be, what never was.

Write. Write till your hands hurt, till your mouth is dry. Write past the running out of words. Write past the pointlessness and the not knowing what to say. Write until you remember. Write until it makes sense. Write until it doesn't make sense anymore. Write until you forget.

Write about being nineteen and getting drunk on martinis and pretending to be grown up. Write about the words your ex-best friend said to you. How she said you were a writer and you told her no. You haven't been writing much anymore.

You haven't been writing because there is nothing to say. Ever since he stripped you naked and shoved dry fingers inside you. There are no words for it. You couldn't write about the pain or the shock or the way you laughed and danced around his room naked. The way you let him become your boyfriend. The way you decided that you must have liked it. You were fifteen. He was eighteen. He was your friend and he was supposed to be a good one. Write about how you never called it rape. You couldn't find the words for it.

Write about the things you would write in the margins of your diary. "Back thoughts" you called them. The things that didn't fit into the narrative, that didn't quite make sense. Write about the fear you know deep down. The terror there isn't words for.

Write like razor blades and beer bottles and smashed glass and blood. Write like one night stands and lost condoms and puke. Write like weed smoke and black eyes and I'm sorry I'm sorry I'm sorry. Write like you're so fucked up when you drink no one wants to be around you. Write like suicide attempts and liquid charcoal and getting formed. Write like I want to live I just don't know how.

Write to know how. Write a love letter to the future. Write away the impossible pain. Write the hope which blisters and burns. Write tomorrow. Write today.

Write the letter that you wanted to receive, the words you needed to hear. Write that love unconditional. Write that witnessing. Write that it wasn't your fault and it never should have happened. Write that it's okay, you fucked up, you can try again.

Write the honest truth, the messy overflow, the silence. Write what wasn't said. Write what you remember. Write the gaping holes where memory should be. Write I'm sorry. Write I'm not sorry. Write I did the best I could with what I had and now I'm trying to do better.

Write it out. Write it down. Write a new world into being. Write a place for the pain. Write a second chance. Write possibility into action. Write the night skies reflecting starlight on black water.

Write the words: I'm still alive.

Dead Raccoon on the Highway

I sit next to him on a park bench on a cool summer day. His smile is beautiful. He tells me I am gorgeous. I take the compliment, wrap it up and put it in my bra, the place that is closest to my heart. So, I am gorgeous. I have succeeded at the task of being beautiful. I have made myself desirable and I am pleased. My heart is still beating, beaten and the sounds of shimmering sentences fill the space between silences. I am trying to stay in this moment. I am kissing a man who I described to my friend as too sexy for his own good. And that is good, it's good, it's good. I will remember this later. I will lie in my bed alone and try to relive the desire. I will conjure it up like a ghost and I will make pathetic love to it.

There is a dead raccoon on the highway. Flies eating at its rotting corpse. A beautiful creature laid to waste from daring to risk movement from one place to another. Crossing the land cut to pieces by roadways. Animals killed by families in cars going on a trip to the cottage. The raccoon runs across the highway in frozen time. Struck. Killed. I don't know why this comes to mind but I see the gathering flies and the raccoon now dead on the highway. I see the yellow lines painted like stiches. I see the impression of a tire flattening the animal's middle. My body is not a dead raccoon. My body is not roadkill. I am a human being having a human experience. It has nothing to do with an animal's life senselessly cut short on the highway.

The sunlight and shade mingle on his face. He is eager, coaxing me with promises of pleasure held subtly in the way he says his words. I am barely here. My hands touch his skin trying to feel the softness. This is better than nothing. It is better that I still try to feel something, even if the feeling is fleeting. It's a little nourishment. I have felt nothing for so long. His smile remains beautiful, my heart remains beaten, ghosts remain ghosts and I still try. I lean over; admire the mole on his neck, the stubble on his face, the exact shade of his hair and his green brown eyes. He certainly is too sexy for his own good. My enjoyment is like a dancing skeleton, a spectacular spectacle, a spectre. Nothing at all.

First Dates

Riding my bicycle next to him, I remain torn between worlds. Neither here exactly nor there. I wonder whose fault it is and I think it must be my own. I'm questioning everything. He asks me what I mean when I say all my friends are queer and I give him some answer like, "We are politicized. We reject heteronormativity and we interrogate it for its roles in oppressive systems like colonialism, capitalism and white supremacy." He says his friends are queer but not like that and I ask him what he means. He says they are less aggressive about it.

I wonder how I have been aggressive but I take his word for it that I have. I want him to invite me over to his place. I want to see what the insides look like. I want to sit on his couch and sleep in his bed and seep my presence into the sheets. He tells me a story about another first date and how he invited the girl over and she started doing coke in his living room. It made him uncomfortable. I want him to invite me over so that on his next date with the next girl he can tell her about me.

He can tell her he went on this date with this aggressive feminist who really had no sense of humour. I have no reason to believe he would say these things.

He asks me if I think the differences between the sexes are biological. I find the question boring and irrelevant and I want to talk about other things. I opened the door by saying I'm a feminist so now we have to discuss this. He talks to me about cave men and testosterone and male aggression. He is wedded to these things. I don't care about them. I want to talk about construction and community, critical analysis, possibility. Or maybe I just want to talk about the sky changing shades above us, deepening its blues. Maybe I just want to lay my head on his shoulder and breathe out a long sigh.

Nothing to Do With Me

I am drawn to bodies of water like lines drawn in sand. I walk to water's edge and stare ahead.

I learned to love, not the sky with its abundance, not the earth. I learned to love boys and men who hurt me, ignored me, touched me in ways I didn't like. I learned to love them, worked hard on the erection of their pedestal which stood upon buried bodies of older desires. I learned to be good, complacent, compliant, pliable, desirable.

My back is a sidewalk, my vagina a swimming pool, my eyes dead fish floating on the surface of the water. I am a million dead things. I am the remainder and I do not remain. I am captured, tamed.

I learned to like it, as we do. I memorized the language. I learned the way to speak, to move. When I stepped out of line I was punished, reminded.

Maybe I don't want this, I think to myself as I am caught up in some kind of sexual act. Maybe this has nothing to do with me.

I am bored. The ceiling is more interesting than his face buried in my pussy, because it could be any pussy, and this is not about me. He thinks he is good at it because he knows what his ex-girlfriend liked and this is not about me.

I am a seashell, a tiny grain of sand, a falling star, a smooth marble counter top. I am the patterns of flowers in gardens. I am nothing. I don't exist.

I walk to the water's edge where nothing else exists either, where there is no need to make sense. I take the heart, unearthed, and I drop it in the water.

II. I COULD NOT SAY WHAT I FELT FOR YOU

Kathleen

We took the back road
a mile walk to the corner store
sprawled on the grass
licking ice cream cones

For years I was angry
when you talked about boys

I learned to talk about them too
cultivated crushes because
I knew it was important to you

We grew older
I moved from sharing your bed
to sleeping on the floor beside it

You were slipping away

School dances found us
pressed against boys
Love songs left me without language

I could not say what I felt for you

Cheap Hotel Room

I want to kiss his neck
but I don't dare
There are stars tattooed there
I ask him to take his shirt off
I suck his dick as best I can
Wanting more

I split moments wide open
drink the juice they drip
I let my fingers search
in dark places
for answers to questions
I don't dare ask

He says lie down
Pressing my legs apart, prying
I am unready and longing
His smell makes me want
but there are no words

It is over before
I have begun

Swarm

On my back ceiling staring

Every ceiling I've known
stares back at me

My heart is a swarm an infestation

Keep the door locked
the windows tightly sealed

You Already Know

Vast summer sky
turned dark with night
offers a hard compassion

A billboard scrawled with graffiti
seen through the window
of a moving streetcar
reads
You already know

Silently, I beg the night
please don't make me choose

Can poetry hold
the anxious thoughts of lovers?
Can the brave moon withstand
all unanswered questions?

The Night, My Own

Tree-lined streets
stark, still

Light pollution
blanketing stars
beneath dull orange-grey

Unafraid and enlivened
by the cover of darkness

I take the long way
home

Round

My mouth
cups the vowel
It is sweet
between my lips
like water
I surround
encase
the sound
Devour
I want
till wanting
sours

III. WILD HEARTS

Coe Hill, Toronto

I used to be Coe Hill, the Canadian Shield, where rocks jut out of earth like exposed bone. It was dynamite that broke them down creating roadways like dry rivers to goldmines with no gold. Coe Hill with its roads and cold lakes named after dead relatives of mine and ancient farm equipment lying in unfarmed fields like dinosaur bones flaking with rust, eroded by sunlight. Coe Hill where the horses run like wild horses unfenced by fences and swim in the lake like children, their joy expressed through their good strong muscles and the way they look at each other with their wide, round eyes. Coe Hill and the wood stove in winter. The wild flowers in spring.

Now I am Toronto, fast and crowded, grey and full of bursts of colour, anonymity and constant exposure, rush hour. Toronto with its sidewalks and hard edges and me still dazzled by city lights, even after all this time. I am Toronto the way a lover can never know the way they are beheld by their beloved, a belonging that fits so right but is still secondhand, still someone else's. Toronto, like the places you can wander into, strange and heated on cold days, parks offering relief from unforgiving cement, the rumbling of bright red streetcars, feeling both lost and found, at home in a crowd.

More home to me than home ever was. A pigeon, more majestic than a hawk. Greater than all the buildings that surround us, that unwanted bird, so loved, so hard to get rid of.

Muses

For Jordyn

She puts ice cubes in her coffee. I put cream in mine. We both leave the sugar alone. When the waitress asks if we want refills we say yes. We punctuate our sentences with fits of laughter. There is something comfortable about us laughing together.

We talk about art. We discuss our creative processes. She is a painter. We consider inspiration, discipline. She tells me about the way she works, the hours spent mixing shades. She tells me about when it comes easy and when it is hard. I love the way she looks when she talks about her art. Her eyes are focused. She comes alive.

We talk about her boyfriend. He hasn't been calling her enough lately. She wonders if he is just getting comfortable or if he is losing interest. She is feeling needy and neurotic. She wants to get laid.

We talk about my ex-boyfriend. He is self-absorbed and has no boundaries. We agree I might have bad taste in men.

I tell her she is not the most neurotic person in the world and she takes it as a compliment.

We talk about trauma. Addiction. PTSD. These things are difficult to talk about but they work their way into the conversation effortlessly.

I stare off into space for a moment. She asks me what I'm thinking so I try to explain. I like that my admissions are not shocking, the way she takes them like she takes her coffee and returns them with some of her own.

At her apartment I pose for her and she takes my picture. She wants me turned that way, she wants me screaming, she wants my arms wrapped around myself, she wants me on the floor. I follow her direction. I don't see the pictures but she tells me they are good. She wants to capture my sadness. I want her to capture my sadness. I want it to be made tangible, visible, separate from myself. She calls me her muse.

I try to relax. I don't try to be beautiful but I hope I am. I watch her face as she reviews the pictures with pleasure. I love the way our laughter, erupting, smoothes the rough edges. I sit on the floor and look up at her, letting my face be my face, letting my body be my body, letting myself be her muse.

I return home wanting to write. I write her smile, the sound of her voice which I hear in my head, the way I sense her power when she takes my picture. I write the way she puts ice cubes in her coffee, the way she isn't getting the attention from her boyfriend she deserves, the way she is an artist, the way she is my muse.

Wild Hearts

For Amy

We are wild, (self)centred. We are exploding, unapologetic. We are wise in our mistakes, carving out the edges of the next catastrophe. We aren't trying hard enough, but oh god how we try.

We lie in bed at night and stare at ceilings. We text message each other to talk about our feelings. The past is gone. It no longer exists. The future stretches, ominous. But it too does not exist.

We share with each other the secrets at our disposal. We are best friends.

We don't drink anymore. Guzzled down too many bottles, took too many pills. We don't party like we used to but now even the sidewalks glitter; there is beauty in everything we do. There is this aching beauty in conversations over coffee as we sort out one thing from another. We listen to each other. We try to live.

We are punished by hope. Our fingers trace the edges of handwritten letters. We want to take what happened and bury it in the ground.

We tell each other how much we love each other. When we embrace we hold on tight. There is a shared understanding that all we have is tonight. We have already destroyed everything else.

Wreckage we know well. We don't glamourize it. But we aren't weighted by it, aren't possessed or consumed by it. With each other we are feathered, our wings stretch out and the wind lifts them. We glide across the smooth expanse of sky.

With each other we remember divinity, that thing no bad deed can ever take from us. We are sorry for what we've done.

We were ravaged. We rolled down hills and spun in circles till we fell over. We watched the horizon moving further and further away. We loved razor blades the way other people love their pets. We sat on the floors of bathrooms more times than we can count.

We are emblazoned. When we look each other in the eye we mean it. We love each other the way only sober addicts can, with that intimate knowing of nothingness and that utter awe at anything. We are somehow born again.

Skate Park

I'm at the skate park trying to look inconspicuous with my neon tights, my bright red hair. I love the smack the wheels make when they impact with the smooth ground.

I want to get better at skateboarding. I want to learn a thing or two from observing the skaters. I'm not good but I'm persistent. I can almost ollie.

I want to belong in this synchronized chaos, the crashing cacophony, an orchestra of movement and sound. I love the way pain is not a deterrent. I want to be fearless. I want to make it look effortless like they do.

I am aware that my femininity sets me apart. I don't want inclusion at the price of who I am. If I ever belong here, I want it to be because I've managed to get a trick or two down. I am not here to learn how to blend in.

I have a friend. We skate here sometimes. The two of us working on our skating in an ocean of masculinity are a massive subversion. We queer the fuck out of this skate park.

She doesn't live in the city, so often I come alone. I work on my ollie consistently and am most often greeted with a cold silence, the occasional flirtatious remark that borders on sexual harassment and the even rarer useful piece of information: put your back foot on the lip, yeah there, that's the sweet spot, it'll work better if you're in motion, bend those knees.

I love the moments when I am treated like just another skater trying to learn a trick. I love the recognition of the skill I have developed and my willingness to learn. I love the insider information, the breakdown of movements.

There is one guy who has been welcoming. He always says hi when I arrive at the park. He passes on useful information.

He and I are sitting on the ledge at the edge of the skate park, sweating and drinking water after a solid session of working on tricks. To our right stretches a grassy park with benches and people doing their summertime things. There is a young woman who is walking through the park collecting garbage.

She bends to reach another piece of trash. My skater friend's eyes watch her body. I say nothing.

He looks at me and says "What?"

"Nothing." I didn't say anything and the last thing I need is to jeopardize this budding friendship with my feminist ways. But it's too late. It's already happening.

He tells me she looks hot in those denim cut offs and that she obviously knows guys are going to check out her ass; why else would she bend over. He tells me I couldn't possibly understand because I don't find women attractive.

I tell him I'm queer and I do find women attractive, but it's a turn-off to feel my desire is an invasive one, that the person I'm attracted to is unaware of or non-consenting to my gaze.

I wish I wasn't telling him these things. I wish we weren't having this conversation and we were instead discussing the details of getting the ollie down.

Fuck It, Let's Go to the Beach

If I had a lover here with me I would take their lead, following any crazy suggestion they made. But I am alone.

I untangle myself from the weak embrace of my blankets and I clamber through the darkness for the light switch. In a rush I dress and get my bike. I get out of the house where the streetlights are still on and morning hasn't quite come.

I ride through darkness, south and west, south and west, toward the water. I ride over a large empty bridge in darkness, alone. No one knows where I am.

I find the beach, perfect in barely morning blue.

Lake Ontario, wide and vast, stretches to the sky. The sand is littered with garbage, a beer bottle left over from someone else's idea of a good time.

It is just me in my pink rain boots, the seagulls, ducks, and swans. The light gradually rises as the day becomes itself.

IV. LIKE A BLADE

Lake

pencil
dive

so
deep
you
don't
have
breath

to
make
it
back

(E)strange(d)

Strange like birds
without flight

Ancestors who once
belonged to skies
have forgotten them

Returned to land
the way whales
who once walked
returned to sea

Ellipsis

The nurse
with her notepad
asks if it is *sharp,*
throbbing, aching,
stabbing

I am present
only to pain

There is no time
no distinction
between inside
outside

The clear bag of
demerol hangs

offering little
relief

Third Wheel

Between you
and yourself
I wasn't much
I was the glue
that brought
you together
the courage
you needed to
see yourself
better the
light you shone
on hidden
parts of you
Yet I loved
you anyway
the way that
punctuation
must love
the sentences
it structures
the way the
window must
love the sky
it frames
I wanted you
to see me

I wanted to be
particular but
I wasn't I was
a function
not a person
an action not
a beloved a
third wheel
when it was
just us two

Break Up

Her smile coaxing miles
of memories from his mind
effectively erasing me
leaving me lost in that
throb of pain he feels
when he finds
something of mine
I left behind

Liminality

Post office boxes. Hotel rooms. Tattoo shops. Hallways.

Where I was and where I'm going leave me where I am. Between.

Elevators. Construction sites. Emergency rooms. Tunnels.

There are sounds in the hall I have yet to recognize, name.

Airports. Trains. Sleep. Loss of virginity.

Lack of distinction causes panic, being in between.

Waiting rooms. Envelopes. Bridges. Car rides.

We don't look into the face of death. We don't contemplate it.

Break ups. Blackouts. Pregnancy. Doorways.

We see it as an ending, a blunt severing. Not the surface of a lake.

Inspiration. Divine intervention. Nervous breakdown.

Split

I walk the water's edge
with empty hands
obsessed with limits
that delineate
this from that

Wondering where
I am divided
which parts were
severed

Which pieces
are no longer
part of the whole

Like a Blade

Rain dampening
darkening sidewalks
Emptiness thundering
with miraculous weight

I have a bag full of books
a bicycle
a racing heart

Stillness which I surrender to
Shuddering silence

Hope that is at once
unlike a blade
and like a blade

V. THE SIZE OF A BIRD

The Size of a Bird

Now, I kiss him on the lips. When I kiss my lips make a sound. His kisses are silent. So I kiss him, making a sound. I pull on his t-shirt and I kiss his lips which are a dull shade of purple. He tastes like coffee and cigarettes. He is soft and smooth. His breath quickens as I touch him. I worry I can't keep up. My desire is slower. It does not arrive on time. I kiss his neck. His jawbone. I use my fingers to press on his collarbone, gently, feeling the edges. There are so many bones in his body, wrapped as they are in his touchable skin. He calls me good. I say *That's what you said yesterday*. He says *You are so good to me*. I have only met him twice. I laugh. I say *No I'm not I just tell you stories about bugs*. The cicada is still singing in the trees. The size of a bird. Do you know what I mean? My favourite part is when he puts his hand over my hand. It's strange what will turn me on. Yes, please, hold my hand in yours. My hand is like a little shell, like a living creature, the size of a bird.

His Adoration

My body is broken into pieces, punished for its existence, segmented into parts of varying relevance. I become a project, an object with symbolic worth, like a coin.

His eyes catch reflected light and dazzle me. His hands look as though they might touch me. I am tense with expectation and desire.

This love he shows me, this adoration that occasionally breaks across my sky, is no substitute for the sweet, cool dirt beneath my feet. I know. Yet I seek to be a cup and him the water. I seek to be a frame and him the window.

His eyes lose focus, look through me.

My breath is like a bird beating wings against a barred cage but I maintain composure.

He is a traveller seeking an open doorway. I am a doorway. He loves me for my welcoming, my shelter.

He is a hunter in search of a kill. He wants good meat for his table. I am that meat. He loves me for my nourishment. My ability to ward off hunger.

I am a cold night. I am a rainstorm. I am the dead of winter.

His love is a lie. I eat it instead of food. I drink it instead of water. I cannot survive.

Ambivalence

The pleasure makes me want to lie down in the road, lie down in the snow, cease everything. He pulls me into the moment with his hands on my body. I feel my body respond, despite myself. My mind is holed up underground, safe. I am exhausted by the pleasure, invaded by it. I want him to touch me, to possess me if only temporarily. I cannot possess myself. Yet my blurred boundaries, so highly prized, disgust me. I want him off me.

He wonders why I don't turn to kiss him but he doesn't stop. I close my eyes, try to like it. Feel the shiver. Try to stick with it but my mind is a cacophony of rage. This ambivalence: I long to come close and I long to pull away.

I want to lose myself in the swamp of pleasure, time muting to a slow river. I want to run, push him off me, grab my bag and run half-dressed out of his apartment, downstairs and out into the cold forgiving air. Gasping like I have been under water.

Do I hurt him with my ambivalence? Have I abandoned myself? Does he hurt me intentionally?

He knows I am beautiful. Beautiful, frozen, unable to move.

Tangle of Veins

Where I live they cover the dirt with cement. Where I live it is frowned upon to sit on the ground. People stare when I stop to touch tree bark, marvelling at texture, when I wrap my arms around the steady, living tree, press my skin to tree skin, breathing together. Where I live we don't walk around with dirt on our faces, we don't put our bare feet in cold water and walk on smooth stone.

The forest calls to me in darkness. I lose my clothes and wander, bare feet on snapping twigs, naked flesh under cover of moonlight, cool air causing tiny hairs to rise.

I listen to the sound of leaves, black against sky, rustling. Trees are not thought to move with agency, animated, but rather to be acted upon by the breeze. This only makes sense if the trees and the breeze are separate phenomenon, denied their unity.

The trees are breathing. The stars blink.

I lie down in the dirt. Insects crawl on me, my skin another surface, another aspect of environment. Leaves entwined in my hair. I cling to the earth like a child, soaking in power. Energy moves through me causing me to vibrate like everything that surrounds me. I pulse in unison. I am reconnected with wholeness, this being which I am.

I am the earth, the sky, the trees. My bones, my veins, they are made of the same. Fingers, arms, branches. I am full of rivers, stars. I am the ocean, still, like I was when I began.

VI. INSISTENCE ON MAGIC

The Deep

Why do we dream of mermaids?
Why do we listen for the siren's wail?
Why this yearning for water?

And the Lord God said unto the serpent
Because thou hast done this, thou art cursed
upon thy belly shalt thou go

And the earth was without form
and void; and darkness was upon
the face of the deep

Beckoning from unfathomable depths
Awakening, remembering, reckoning
Monstrous, familiar, old as time

The Crone on Her Bicycle

The crone
in bright red lipstick

stops her bicycle
at the light

I am standing on the curb
She smiles, says

I love your purple hair
I smile back, she asks

Does it feel good?
I smile, say *Yes*

She beams
That's all that matters

And she takes off
as the light turns green

Lavender

Spot the lavender plant
growing in a garden
Touch, letting scent
linger on fingers

Essential oil, a few drops
in a spray bottle
to use when dusting

A few drops in the bath
A drop on each wrist
On the tip of my nose

Over coffee she hands me
a small glass mason jar

I make a sweet smelling
satchel for when
I am anxious

I leave an offering
on my altar
I make tea

Femmes in Motion

For Jasmin

Skateboarding
down darkening streets

The sounds of wheels
against pavement

Our laughter
mixing together

We break the rules
of what bodies

get to move
in what ways

Soaked

Green, grey, glistening, slippery
I bicycle through city streets
without a back fender

Soak myself through with water
The fabric of my dress turning
darker blue

Laughing, intermittently singing
It's less like riding, more like swimming

The air is thick with heat
The smooth motion of my feet
as they connect with pedals
Wheels spinning

Flight

We were children
watching fairies
make homes
in fallen forest logs

Their capacity for flight
wings catching sunlight
sparkling

Insistence on magic
in the midst of what
we were living with

Fairies remain
despite widespread
disbelief in their
existence

Sheela Na Gig

She smiles
steady gaze

Vulva held
open

Body aged
Pleasure paramount

Passageway
through which
we enter
this world

Fireflies

Living starlight fields

Lit windows of cities sparkle

VII. NEVER ENOUGH

Returning

The Valley spreads wide in the middle of the city. Ribbons of highway razor the land. Drunk and stumbling my feet return me to brown murky water, singing cicada, sunlight bright on pavement.

Face to face with graffitied cement, breathing in summer heat while he fucks me. I am docile, submissive, sexy. I subdue him, make him remember why he keeps me, dull the edge of his rage. Behind my eyelids I keep a little part of me.

I stretch myself across the Valley, become the foxes who come at night, the little bugs which climb tall blades of grass, the wildflowers, abundant, flourishing. I am the trees reaching skyward, growing intricately around each other, reaching for sunlight.

His fucking is done and I am laughing again. I am smiling, am allowed to smile.

I am returning to water, to the light catching on its curves. I am returning to the ducks riding the slow current, the little minnows glinting.

In the Valley time is just the sun coming and going.

Poison

Coffee table covered in empties. The brown glass of beer bottles, precious, the light reflected on their surfaces, reminiscent of the sun. Air cloudy with relentless marijuana smoke. No motivation except to escape. I am dizzied with the night before the hangover, enacting the ritual of intoxication. Getting straight fucked. The night calls to me like all the broken promises I ever believed. I long to find myself in a stranger's bed. I long to forget myself.

I love the heat inside the bottle, the way the bubbly liquid warms me. I was freezing cold, numb like a statue. Now I am animated. I lose my inhibition, my sense of isolation. I lose direction. I float on wave after wave of sensation, to manifest as a marionette, a dead thing walking. The bottles clink, the conversation bubbles, the stars throb like an invitation. I disappear.

Lamp lit streets with sidewalks that lead to bars we are kicked out of. Alleyways feel more and more like home. Blurred faces and belief that everyone is as drunk as me. Laughter at nothing, faith this is everything. Pulled down pantyhose, pissing rivers and trying not to get it on my clothes. The strangers, lovers. Wanting to be touched so much, wanting to feel flesh to flesh. Blowjobs in the bushes outside the bar. Relentless wanting. Give it to me harder. Make me feel anything.

Coming to in a midday morning. Still a little drunk but it's fading. Dizzy, head aching, sick. Not wearing my clothes, piecing together where I am, unsure. I want to laugh. I feel proud of this disaster. A little baffled, a little terrified. I look at the stranger and I imagine a deep, sustaining love. I want to vomit so I ask if there's a bag. Lying in his bed next to him in a pile of disheveled sheets, I dry heave and dry heave, try to get up the poison. I don't have the energy to be ashamed. Standing is too much work. I only hope he will let me stay here for a bit. I can't move.

I place the bag of vomit on the floor next to the bed, slipping in and out of sleep. The vomit drips across the floor. I ask him the questions, try to fill in the blanks. He tells me I am really loud when I get fucked, that I screamed and woke the neighbours. He tells me I met him at the bar, grabbed his arm. He tells me the condom broke. He is laughing. His eyes glitter. I am swimming in a thick sea. His words are coming from very far away.

I listen to the story about this drunk girl he picked up at the bar who is me. I listen to the things she did and said. I never want to see myself again.

Mountains on the Moon

I can write you a million poems dedicated to an endless litany of ex-lovers. You can have them all. But I'm not sure what else I have to say.

I need him to be happy. I need him to tell me my politics are acceptable, maybe even cute. I need him to be enthralled with my eccentricities. He shrugs off my armpit hair like it's no big deal, like his opinion on it matters to begin with. I forget I don't fucking care what he thinks. I forget I am already happy. I don't want or need his approval. I love myself fiercely and unequivocally. I remain wild despite the many cages I willingly enter.

I remain caged despite my wildness.

When my friend asks me how my date went I say okay, I want to see him again. I hope he will invite me over to his house. I remind myself to scope out the scene a little more next time before saying I'm a feminist, to be more careful with that particular gem.

I think I need his approval. I'm not even sure I like him.

As a child I would go out into the night and stare up at the stars, take my dad's binoculars so I could see the mountains on the moon. My heart was hungry, wild, not searching for cages.

I used to go into the forest on my own. The light was filtered green, the river moved between the trees. My hands were dirty and my lungs full.

There are days I can't make myself get out of bed. I don't put that particular piece of information on my internet dating profile.

I want him to say he likes me, I'm pretty, my opinions are interesting, acceptable. I am a liar when I say the date was good, that really, I'm not that kind of feminist. He doesn't have any idea what kind of feminist I am. He is afraid of the word and I am afraid of myself.

Mostly a Mess

I find myself sleeping in the cold in someone else's piss. I am hiding under cardboard because I think I will be safe here.

I turn myself into a spectacle, a story, a back alley. I turn myself into a cockroach infested apartment, a blowjob, a one night stand.

My heart is a broken bottle shattered on cement. Mildly dangerous, but mostly a nuisance, mostly a mess.

Months slip away, dissolving into a blur of years. I tell you stories. Times when my heart felt full to bursting, times when I ran toward the horizon, hungry, famished. I was chasing nothing.

I talk and talk. I watch your face as my words fall on your ears. I want my words to be a stone in a pond. I want to watch the ripples, reaction. I want my words to be a stone against a windshield, coaxing cracks.

I want to believe, like a child with an ear to a tin can on a string, that some part of the message is getting through.

I was certain I would have my own shopping cart. One day, I did. I stole that shopping cart from the grocery store parking lot. I dragged it up three flights of stairs to my tiny apartment. There it sat in my bedroom, a bright yellow shopping cart against a bright blue wall.

I still try to pretend that it meant something. I still want to believe that it meant everything to me.

VIII. THE WORST THING

Yellow Lines

I want to lie
down on the highway
Yellow lines
divide me
Hold me together
like stiches

Had you like a conversation
Broke you like a promise

Your spine, my centrefold
Your fingers, the hands on my clock

Holding your body
as if I were holding
my own self

Furious Blue

The windshield captures sky
the oncoming night
Its furious shade of unwanted blue

We are going nowhere
but at least we are on the move

You drive, I ride
At each crossroad I decide left or right
or straight through

The past is on our trail
The memories we push down
come spilling now

There isn't enough beer
in this whole town
to wash them down

Sexy

It was a cage
A pin pressed through
my wing

It was a target
A red X
like the spray paint
ones

On trees
marked
for cutting down

Key in Hand

We never took the back way
were scolded for walking
alone at night
turned our heads
over shoulders
walked with keys in hand

I could never tell you how it was
The words would be distant
the way history is
It wouldn't be visceral, real
like when your lover
throws you on the floor
the look in his eye
the pressure of his body
the certainty
he will kill you
if you
let him

Rearview

Hindsight isn't 20/20
either love

No matter how many
rearview mirrors
I still choose you
I still gut myself
I still do

The Worst Thing

You are the sound of my breaking
gut wrenching
never knew it could hurt like that pain

You are the worst thing
You are hands on my skin

You were everything

Alleyway

I smash the bottle
fuck goddamnit
glass glittering
on pavement

I suck him off
push fullness
back of throat
choking

Thumb
pressed down
on lighter

Friction
spark

Queer Monstrosity

If sex is always violence
invasive, unwanted

If women, who I desire
are always only desired

If I act on this desire
am I harming them too?

IX. UNBROKEN

Meat

The word *Vagina* is a knife. We talk about rape theoretically, over
our dinner. We discuss the implications of rape in a cool,
detached way and yet my voice betrays me. A fire is burning to cover
darkness which covers what I will not think. We talk about rape
using academic words. We consider whether rape is really sex at all;
I mean it's really more about power. But, I say offhandedly, *while I know
that rape is an act of violence more than it is an act of sex I also know that
my rapist got off on it. It felt good for him. It was pleasurable.* Ejaculation
into my vagina: a horrible sequence of words. I don't remember it.
I will never string together those moments. I will never know, as
I was asked, how long it lasted. He asks me *Is rape a transgression?*
And I say *No. It is a sanctioned act.* I remember him fucking me. I
remember tears. A mattress. Our bedroom. Exhaustion. Terror. Meat.

A Cup of Tea

It is seven a.m. His alarm goes off. He turns onto his side, shuts off the beeping. He is a bicycle courier and it is December. The day ahead is cold, long, wet.

I am nestled in the warmth of our bed, cocooned. I am a university student living on government loans. My class doesn't start until later. The bed is safe and warm.

I am half awake from his alarm. I am aware of his breathing, his movements and this awakens me further, alerting me.

He is annoyed, irritated, thinking of the long hours ahead, the cold dirty slush that will cling to his legs. I want to bury myself further into the safety of the bed, sink into its forgiving depths.

He breaks the silence.

"Get up" he says.

"I don't need to get up. My class isn't until later."

"Get up and make me a cup of tea."

"I'm sleeping."

"Get up."

"Don't do this."

"I have to work. Get me a cup of tea."

"I'm not going to."

My heart is beating fast, pounding out the sound of blood in my ears. The adrenaline is sharp electric fire lighting me up from the inside.

I am stupid. Not picking my battles. Not playing it safe. But I am ready to fight for this, for the warmth of this bed, for the sweetness of sleep. I know already there will be no more sleep.

He rips the blankets off me and throws them against the far wall. We are under water again. His words have that weight to them, the slowness of urgency.

"Get me a cup of tea."

I scramble past him on the floor and steal the blankets back. I know that I will pay for this. I know that it isn't worth it. I know that I will be begging for forgiveness and later, on the floor, I do.

Love Is a Strategy, It Was All I Could Do

He threw the mattress off the third floor balcony. It landed on the front lawn. I couldn't stop him. He pushed me hard. I went through the wall. I couldn't stop him. Time moved quickly. He threw the furniture around the room. Time slowed down unbearably. I tried to change the outcome. I argued with him, pleaded. It was like we were under water. We were caught in an unstoppable flood. Everything was blurred and incoherent. Everything just was and we could not believe that it was.

I was not a battered woman, an abuse victim; those were not the things I was. I was in love. Love was like syrup, like a hot stove I kept touching, a destination at which I could not arrive. Love was a staircase, a smashed guitar, the look on his face. I was not his victim. He was not my abuser. He couldn't be. He twisted my limbs. He cut off my breath. He called me names, made me cry. I couldn't stop him.

I sat in a small room with a police officer. I swore to tell the truth and I told it. A camera recorded my words but the words could not convey. The story could not be told. The crushing love I betrayed by saying, no it cannot be done. I was terrified, exhausted, I didn't know what to do. I told because I didn't want to die.

Grief is a slow process. There is no hurrying it. I was surprised because it didn't hurt so much. After he was gone, I felt okay. I felt numb. I felt fine. It was over. I'd survived. He was gone and I could admit it. That was an abusive relationship. I was a survivor of what they call domestic violence. I didn't cry. I didn't think about it. I just said he put me through the drywall and that was that.

Four months gone and I was at the end of another bottle, at the end of my rope. I had lost all my friends, I had lost my shoes. I was in a valley somewhere bleeding into the grass. He called me names. I couldn't stop him. But then it hit me like a pile of bricks, an avalanche, *if only I had just been good.* If only I had been better. If only I had loved him right. He wouldn't have hurt me. He wouldn't have left me. I loved him. He was in jail and I was alone.

Years passed, bottles added up, experience in courtrooms and police stations turned my story into a worn out repetition. Yes he did. He got on top of me. Wouldn't let me move. Wouldn't let me breathe. It was like this. For this long. They asked me a million questions and made a million suggestions and I tried not to look at him in the courtroom. I had to hide, bury, deny my love.

Because no one would believe me if they knew the truth. No one would believe he had done these things if I admitted I still loved him too.

I loved my abuser. I loved him so much and I hope I never love anyone like that again. All I want is to love like that again. I loved him when he kicked my legs out from under me. I loved him when he kicked me in the stomach while I lay on the floor. I loved him while he slept in my bed at night, when he rode off on his bicycle, when we cooked meals together. I loved his smile, his hands, his voice. I loved him fiercely and he almost killed me and I loved him still. I loved him in the courtroom while I told the jury he raped me and I knew that nothing could make sense again.

In my therapist's office I cried and cried. I told her I loved him.
She said I was experiencing attachment to my abuser. I said he made
me better. She said he was grooming me. My heart sunk because
I could not deny our love. I couldn't believe he didn't love me. It
was the love that made it worth it. It was the love that soothed the
obliterating pain. I had to love him. Why else would I stay? How else
could I make everything okay?

He called me a slut. He screamed in my face. He asked me if I knew
who I was fucking with. He chased me on his bike. He cut the
doorbell off the front of the house. He stole my phone and keys.
He cried in my arms. He said he was sorry. He swore he loved me.
He loved me so much it drove him fucking crazy. I felt like I was
disappearing. I knew I could never let him go. I belonged to him so
he belonged to me. He hurt me. He loved me. I loved him and I still
loved him even after.

My love was how I survived. It kept me alive. It was a strategy.
My grief was the devastating loss of that fantasy, the loss of that love,
and the facing up to the reality of what happened to me. It was no
grand love affair. It was no unbelievable, maddening love that no
one could possibly understand. It was no chaotic, unrelenting,
passionate, possessive love. It was violence. My boyfriend was
extremely abusive to me. I couldn't stop him. It was not safe to
leave. I faced the prospect of my death, the betrayal of my trust, the
degradation of my spirit, the violation of my body and the terror of
violence. And so I loved him. I loved him so it made sense.

With a heart overflowing, aching with the pain of an unbearable
love, I took a shoebox taped shut out into a field in the dead of a
witnessing night. That shoebox held the lie, two photo albums which
proudly displayed the happiness of our unbelievable love. On my

hands and knees I dug a hole in the dirt; under the certain moon I dug a grave. I was devastated. My heart kicked and screamed. I wouldn't believe. I couldn't believe. And I loved him. Fiercely. Endlessly. It was the only thing I knew. I put the box in the earth. I buried our love. Alone, in the night, I cried the tears I could never cry. I started the process of letting it die.

Suicidal Ideation

I think about dinosaur bones. I contemplate suicide. I think about
bridges. I could jump off. I think of city skylines, Toronto, its heights.
I think of pigeons, flight.

A dull, aching pain rises and falls. The doctor asks me how my mood
is and for how many days I have been depressed. The problem is I
can't keep track of days, they run together, one blurring into the next.
It seems like forever but I have no idea. I have no point of reference.

When I was seventeen I used to fall asleep in the bathtub with my
nose above the surface of the water, hoping I would drown. I would
take some pills to help me sleep. I would wake up freezing and
pruned, still alive. I would think about baking myself a cake filled
with poison.

I think about lakes, deep and bottomless, with smooth, glass
surfaces. I think about seaweed and sea monsters, nightmares,
unmentionable things. I think about sewing rocks into my clothes,
wading into the water.

I climb staircases in private. I take the time to be alone. I find public
washrooms and lock myself into the stall. No one can see me here.

When I am hopeful I write on the wall. It's the truth telling, even to
perfect strangers, that gives me hope. It's the secret interaction, the
soul telling, that humility of witnessing another's deepest secrets in
a bathroom stall. I write down things I can't say, things I can't tell
anyone. I can't tell anyone how much I want to die.

Suicidal ideation. I am careful to answers the question *No* when I am asked if I have thoughts of suicide. Do I think about killing myself? Do I have a plan? Have I ever been hospitalized for a suicide attempt?

I attempt to escape. I see the tree branches lying on the ground, cast down by some storm and I take a picture. They remind me of bars on cages, of window ledges, broken things on the sidewalk. I attempt to explain, if only to myself, what living means, what dying would mean.

I sleep for days and listen to the same song over and over. I have found a steady place, a steady pace and I do not want to disturb it. I don't tell anyone. When I am asked how I am doing I say I am doing fine. When I am asked what I did yesterday, what I am doing tomorrow, I fumble. I am trying to stay alive.

I think about the bodies of animals killed on the road by cars rushing by. I think about the driver and wonder if they felt a quick, painful dagger to the heart as they recognized the thump of their wheels going over the injured animal. Or if they felt indifference, annoyance, nothing. I think about the animal bleeding out on the road alone.

When I was fifteen a boy in my school told me that I didn't really want to die because if I did I would just do it already. I didn't have the courage to try until I was really drunk and even then I chickened out and drank shampoo to try to get the pills up. I went to the hospital. They gave me charcoal instead.

If I don't want to die, if I won't really do it, then why do I think about it so much?

Time spreads out like a terrible promise. I can't even take my own life.

I think of horizons where sky and water meet. I think about bricks used to make buildings. I contemplate the various shades of grey. I think about sharp edges, knives, being murdered, that moment when you know for sure you are going to die.

These are not morbid thoughts. This is not morbid contemplation. I am holding up the impermanence of my being, my body, and looking at it. I am wondering what keeps me here and what would make me go.

I don't want to die. I lie on the floor and I pretend it's the ceiling and I cry until I can't cry anymore. I lie in abject exhaustion but I am not even tired because all I do is sleep. I am heartbroken. I do not know why.

My options feel like death and sleep, drunkenness and razor blades, oblivion and oblivion. I hate the sound of my own voice, the thoughts in my head. I hate my cowardice, my pain, my inability to kill myself. I love myself the way I love the waves in the ocean. I am awed, terrified. I want to dive in. I want to run away. I hate myself because I am an unbroken horse, a wild one. I love myself because I still don't want to die.

I don't want to die. I have failed at life and death but I have not failed at failure. In terms of failure, I am a success. Breath. It moves through me relentlessly even after all of this. My desire for death is not pathetic. My inability to really want it is not pathetic. I think about lakes because I am brave. I want to drown because I think my heart is at the bottom of the lake. I am still alive. I have not died.

I think about the seasons and the gradations of shades which make up sky. I think about the skeletons of birds, the decaying leaves, the cool breeze. I think about hope, a burning, glowing, aching, undeniable presence, another chance and another one. I think about suicide and even after all of this time I am still alive. I lie on the floor. I am still alive.

I write the words I am still alive.

Acknowledgements

The first version of this manuscript was written in 2013. So many people have come in and out of my life since then, supporting me, changing me, inspiring me. Like all work, this work was created in relationship. My gratitude is endless and cannot adequately be summed up here.

I would like to thankInanna Publications for believing in this book, the anonymous reviewers who provided valuable feedback, and Cee Lavery for the beautiful cover design. I would like to thank my loved ones: Jordyn Taylor, Jasmin Fahd, Holly Jo, Casey Jean, Ash Baksi, Elyse Lue-Mayo, Amy Saunders, Jay Manicom, and Daria Davydova, to name only a few. I would like to thank the communities which sustain and uplift me: my fellow alcoholics and addicts, my fellow survivors, and my fellow queers.

This book was written on Anishinabek, Haudenosaunee, and Wendat land.

Clementine Morrigan is a writer, artist, and working witch. She writes the zine *Fucking Magic*. Their first book, *Rupture*, was published in 2012. Their creative writing has appeared in the literary journals *Prose & Lore* and *Soliloquies,* and her scholarly writing has appeared in the academic journals *Somatechnics, The Canadian Journal of Disability Studies*, and *Knots*. They have also written for *Guts Magazine* and *Shameless Magazine*. She is the creator of two short films, *Resurrection* (2013) and *City Witch* (2016). Their creative, artistic, and scholarly works consider trauma, madness, addiction, sobriety, gender, sexuality, desire, magic, re-enchantment, environment, and more-than-human worlds. She facilitates workshops and guest lectures on a number of topics. They provide professional tarot reading services for individuals and events. She is a white settler of Irish, Scottish, and English ancestry living in Tiohtià:ke/Montréal. They are a practitioner of trauma magic. To learn more about her work please visit clementinemorrigan.com.